where are the rebels?

where are the rebels?

joseph ridgwell

Ternary Editions
New York

where are the rebels? © 2018 by Joseph Ridgwell

All Rights Reserved. Printed In the United States of America. No part of this text or art may be used or reproduced in any manner whatsoever without permission from the author, except in the case of brief quotations embodied in critical articles and reviews.

SECOND EDITION

Where are the Rebels? was originally published by Blackheath Books as *Where are the Rebels?* (© 2008) and *Load the Guns* (© 2009) and were edited by Geraint Hughes. Both were published in editions limited to 100 signed copies.

ISBN-13:   978-1-937073-74-9

TERNARY
EDITIONS

29 Sugar Hill Road
North Salem, NY 10560

www.ternaryeditions.com

CONTENTS

Load the Guns	9
Ode to Beer	10
Footsteps in the Rain	11
Kings Cross At 6 AM	12
Where are the Rebels?	14
Ode to Nedra Talley	15
The Young Die Screaming in the Land of Broken Dreams	17
Wasted Life Blues	18
Ode to Estelle Bennett	19
Genevieve	21
The Last Night with You	22
The Singer of Sal	23
In Search of the Lost Elation	24
A Recurring Image	25
Heroism of the Longneck	26
Ode to Alexandra Denny	27
Passive	28
Bonnie and Clyde Were Lovers	29
Let the Good Times Roll	31
The Kiss	32
Just another Day in the Cross	33
To the Girl on the Train	35
Great Day	36
Australia	37
Zippolite (Beach Poem 17#)	38
When I Saw Her	39
30	40
Moonlight in the Gutter	41
Ode to the Air-Guitar Busker of Kings Cross	42
The Corpse	43
More Beautiful than the Night	44
After Sunrise	45
The Roaring Twenties	46

Load the Guns

When the dark is day
And the sun shines nevermore
And a lone bugler
Appears at the end of the street
Playing a melancholy Last Call
That is the time
To load the guns
To load the guns
To walk out of the shack job
To kick the deadbeat partner into touch
To yell in the middle of the road
To howl at the moon
To dance with the devil
And kiss the first person that you meet
Tongues included
And shake the hand of a stranger
Put flowers in your hair
To smile crazily
And remember that you were once young
And the world was once young
And nothing matters anyway
Because death comes to us all

Ode to Beer

Without beer what is there
Are should I say without beer
There is what?
Nothing
Beer is all there is
Rivers of beer
Oceans of the stuff
The amber nectar
The ambrosia of the Gods
The one constant to hang onto
When love is a lie
And dreams never come true
And money is made out of paper
And all the things you once believed in
Turn out to be false
So come on drink up, drink up your beer
There's bound to be some more if you want it
I know I do

Footsteps in the Rain

The bars and pubs
And pints of watery lager
Shiny brass beer pumps
Fruit machines and fluorescent shots
False camaraderie
Stinking urinals
Just a battered boozer from the East End
Walking in the fucking rain
Holes in your shoes
Jobless and joyless, but not defeated
Still youngish, still hopeful, still upbeat
As the dreams fade away
And the beautiful women don't even see you
And cars flash by like diamonds
While the songs of the innocent play silent arias on your besotted brain
You are a rock, an island of stupidity
The drugs, the clubs, the sweaty dance floors of despair
The early morning mist
Illegal cab drivers
Pimps, ponces, and perverts
The last sad refrain
A cold single bed
Spunked stained quilt
And even those dog eared books and slim volumes of poetry
To protect you from yourself
You are a rock
And nobody knows your name
Like footsteps in the rain.

Kings Cross At 6 AM

I walk the dull and dirty city streets around 6 A.M
Sheets of newspaper blown across the pavement
Appear like mad drunken dancers in a crazed musical
Headlined front page becomes a pissed up Gene Kelly
The T.V Listings a gin soaked Frank Sinatra
Prostitutes catch taxicabs
To return home, fix-up, and rest their aching cunts
Two middle-aged hospital workers walk hurriedly,
heads bowed into the wind
Another ten-hour early shift waiting
The pavements beneath the ATM machines are littered
with hundreds of bank receipts
Like the remains of a ticker tape parade celebrating
the eternal Saturday night
And listlessness hangs in the air
Like the remnants of energy from ten thousand long gone
weekend revelers
The Cross never sleeps
You can grab a beer, a fix and a feed 24/7
But at 6 A.M the place is in a strange flux
Everything animated in a dream like limbo
Drunks stagger along red-faced and glassy-eyed
Oblivious to their immediate surroundings
Junkies, loose-limbed and on the nod, look beat
I observe these scenes, these early morning
Kings Cross Scenes
Until a deluge of devastating sunshine floods the main drag
And for one exquisite moment everything becomes golden
Like a giant cigarette butt
A frozen moment until the gold washes away
Replaced by the heroin light of early morn
The Cross is steeped in junk history
Echoes of former deals and drug highs reverberate off the club,
bar and strip-joint walls
Along with ghostly images of long dead prostitutes and

doomed drug-addicts
Images that prowl the vulnerable Sunday morning streets
As I go gliding down through the debauched and
exploited decades
Back eventually to a brighter time
When Aboriginal people sat on hilltops overlooking
Sydney harbour
Discussing the dreamtime, going fishing, and
making stencils of their handprints
A million sun-filled days ago.

Where are the Rebels?

Where are the rebels?
Now that days are long
And nights short
As I think of those who died
And those still alive
And those yet to be born
And those never to be born
So pass the wine
And fuck everything
And don't be afraid of the dark
Be afraid of the morning
For the morning brings the truth
Those lines around your starry eyes
Crows feet
And as the sun rises
I raise my beer and ask
Where are the rebels?

Ode to Nedra Talley

Here's an ode to Nedra Talley
A member of the legendary Girl group
The Ronettes
Who I first heard as a love-struck teenager
Tuning in every night to Randal Lee Rose's
Late night shift on Capital Gold
And what music that man played
Ending each show with Tommy McClain's heart-breaking version of
Sweet Dreams
While in between you had Frankie Lymon and the Teenagers,
Dion and the Belmonts, Maureen Gray, Randy and the
Rainbows, The Crystals, The Mystics, The Earls, Rosie
and the Originals, Rudy and the Romantics, The Coasters,
The Teen Queens
One rocking solid gold tune after another
While all my friends were listening to Darlek music
And popping low-grade ecstasy
In gloomy, dirty warehouses
It was the era of dance music
Apparently
To be sociable, I went a few times, and felt the rush of the love dove
But immediately sensed it's superficial, chemical, artificial nothingness
I saw through it all
But none of that mattered
Because I had Randal Lee Rose
Every night
And during one such show I caught The Ronettes
For the very first time
With the earth-shattering vocals of Veronica Bennett
Sand-blasting my eardrums
Making the hairs on my neck stand up on end
like porcupine quills

A teenage symphony coming at me over the airwaves
Like a radical musical missile
Exploding soul, glamour, and teenage angst
All over me
I listened again and again, and again
And then I had to see those girls, to know what they looked like
And I did
I chanced upon a TV documentary of the Sixties
Showing the girl-group in their heyday
In all their classical pomp
And I heard the voice and saw the sister
But it was the cousin that caught my attention
Shimmying to the left of Ronnie
Oohhing and Ahhhhing
Giving it all she had
And I fell in love with her
It was Nedra
I wanted to be with
And when she sang Baby I Love You
I told her I loved her right back
For it was me she was talking to
And afterwards I made it my mission in life to find out
What happened to Nedra
After all those years
It took a while
But I found out
She got married, had kids, and became a born again Christian
Sadly for me the unrequited love affair was over
But I still had the music
So fare thee well
Nedra, Ronnie and Estelle
You may have changed
But the music never did.

The Young Die Screaming in the Land of Broken Dreams

Taking toilet breaks
To go for a wank
Out of sheer boredom
At work
While the
Young
Die
Screaming
In
The
Land
Of
Broken
Dreams
Is what kills us all
You and I
And the man in the moon
And the bum on the hill
As the sun gets hotter
Or nearer
And will one day explode and destroy everything.

Wasted Life Blues

It was certainly a pathological sadist
Who invented the working week
For eight hours a day, Monday to Friday
Is certainly far too much time
For any job to occupy
Even with all those crazed managers
Handing out pointless tasks like confetti
So what exactly do you do?
At work
To piss away the time
To make those eternal hours fade away like a long lost lover
Or a sad and beautiful sirens song
Stare at paperclips
One sentence emails
Surf the web
Think about lunch
Talk endlessly about absolutely nothing
Conduct an office affair
Pretend to be ambitious
Harbour visions of successive promotions
Tell them what they want to hear
Delegate, procrastinate, obfuscate
Or maybe you bide the endless minutes
Hours
Days
Months
Years
Even decades
Re-enforcing and vigorously policing systems
Invented by the clinically insane
The power hungry, the demented, the greed and war mongers
An easily subjugated automaton
Unconsciously recording a soundless symphony
Of your own personal death drive
A tuneless libretto of wasted life blues

Ode to Estelle Bennett

One third of the 1960's most memorable girl group
Was a petite and pretty girl
By the name of Estelle
Older sister to Veronica
And cousin to Nedra
Ah the Ronettes
Even today I only have to hear the first bars of
Be my Baby
To once again be a teenager in love
And dreaming of a kiss
But fame for Estelle was fleeting
For while her sister married Phil Spector
And her cousin found God
Estelle was left with nothing
But memories of a stratospheric rise to stardom
As brief as it was dramatic
And when the group broke-up in 1966
Estelle simply disappeared
So where did she go when the fairy tale ended
When the glamour and glitz faded to dust and ashes
When the photographers, magazines, and hacks stopped calling
When the fickle fans moved onto the next big thing
The girl who fashioned the unforgettable look
The big, big, big, hair
Tight-fitting dresses
And all that mascara and Cleopatra eyeliner
Some say she lost her mind
Some say her heart was broken
And in later years
Could be found wandering the streets
Of New York City
While the ghosts of former lovers
Besieged her tormented soul
Sleeping rough
Homeless

Telling random strangers
That she was Estelle of the Ronettes
And would be performing in a nearby jazz club
That evening
Before finding a sheltered doorway
And laying her head down
As stars shone from up on high
And for every kiss you'd give her
She'd still give you three.

Genevieve

Is sitting in a battered white Lloyd Loom chair, legs parted
White knickers, nylon's, and black suspenders
Creamy white thighs
She is smoking a Cuban cigar
Romeo y Julieta
And waiting for me
I bought the chair in a second-hand shop in Colombia Road
Where the Sunday Flower Market is held
And I'm just down the road in a Bethnal Green boozer
The pub is deserted and dying
And I'm thinking of Genevieve, waiting for me
In the paper-mache sofa, peeling paint, and gilded splinters
With her legs parted, fleshy resolute thighs,
And the cigar, creating elegant plumes of grey smoke
Outside, the night is dark and filled with sadness
I walked hurriedly, head bowed to the wind
Towards my love, towards my doom, towards my everything.

The Last Night with You

It was a cheap motel somewhere, but nowhere
Cockroaches dancing along the windowsills
Outside the nocturnal sounds of the city
You were fast asleep, snoring ever so gently
I ran my fingers through your hair
And gazed at your sleeping face
You looked content, like an angel baby
I carefully peeled away your arms and legs
And climbed out of the bed and over to the window
You sighed like a child and turned your back
Symmetrical shoulder blades revealed in blue light
I looked out of the window
And smoked a cigarette
Outside I saw a cat hugging the walls
And knew I was going to lose you
And it that it would be our very last night together
And as the night faded to grey
My heart exploded into a million shimmering fragments

The Singer of Sal

That sultry Cape Verdean night
Lobster and strong Island wine
Sound of the Atlantic all around
The coast of West Africa a distant dream
Me and the Belle
Celebrating something
Our first holiday abroad
Well, we'd always been poor
But unlike old rich people
We were young and free and still looking to the future
The restaurant was empty
Inside and out
I didn't mind
But felt sorry for the singer
Playing his lonely tunes
On the wooden decking there
The stars out and the ocean roar
A cool breeze blowing
We made requests
The singer joined us at our table
Told us all about his big trip to New York
The grogue was brought out
We talked, smoked, and drank the night away
Our room only a few hundred feet away
How we got there I'll never know
And the next day
Just after noon
I saw the singer man of Sal
He didn't look so good
And neither did I
We smiled
Didn't stop to speak
For we both knew
What's gone is gone
And can never be brought back.

In Search of the Lost Elation

So now
I stand all alone
But somewhere
Out there
Is the lost elation
All I have to do
Is find it.

A Recurring Image

Lately I have been dreaming of a
Recurring image
In the image I am twenty-five
Wearing sandals, long shorts,
And a white tee-shirt
That has printed on the back, the words
Journey for the Endless Schooner
I am in Oxford Street, Sydney, Australia
The sun is shining
In the image I am walking away from myself and smiling
Walking away into the hazy days of the future
And in the blinking of an eye
It is ten years later
And I am thirty-five
And no longer smiling
But I like this recurring image
For it reminds me of how short our lives are
And how late it is
Much later than you think.

Heroism of the Longneck

Swigging from those long necked bottles
At the El Alamain fountain
Or outside Riteway
Wasting days
Just waiting for something to happen
But nothing ever did happen
And yet there was always the bottle
Seven hundred and fifty millilitres of booze
Dripping across the lips and tongue
And down the gullet
Raising the arm
The long shadow at 90 degrees...

Ode to Alexandra Denny

'Help me,' were Sandy's last words
And sometimes I think about that desperate plea
As I play her records
Late at night, after a few beers
The voice clear and pure like a mountain stream
Or an endless azure sky
Or the memory of something once forgotten
The sound of innocence, so sweet and true
And then the death
Falling down the stairs
And hitting her head on hard stone slabs
And the stupidity of the mother
For refusing to take her own daughter to hospital
Because she was embarrassed to be seen with a drunk
Well, all that long ago shit hardly matters
For the beautiful voice was already fading like a forgotten summer
So on monochrome days or pale evenings
I think about charismatic people like Sandy
Who burn so brightly
And illuminate all our lives
The writers, poets, and trailblazers
Innovators, artists and musicians
And when the fickle birds head south once again
And the fretful sailors cry out
Does anyone really know where the time goes?

Passive

What kills the soul
And extinguishes the fire
Is passivity
Feeling nothing
Refusing to live
Just existing
From day to day
Until shrouded death
Shows her fleeting face
And beckons you
To go with her

Bonnie and Clyde Were Lovers

Bonnie and Clyde were lovers
And killers of cops
Store owners
And anyone else who got in their way
But Bonnie and Clyde had style
And that is why the myth endures
Because most people don't possess an ounce of style
Politicians don't have style
Nor bankers, pop stars, businessmen or Mayors
And no matter what they do or how they do it
It's instantly forgettable
All of it
I've met hospital workers and street bums with more style than those guys
But Bonnie and Clyde had the most style of all
The way that pretty diminutive woman dressed
And held those pistols with one dainty foot
On the fender of a stolen ford V8 Roadster
Or Clyde with a converted Browning automatic
Slung low and easy across his knees
An angelic smile upon an assassins face
Grainy images impossible to resist
And Bonnie could even get a line down
Another simple thing that most alleged poets find impossible to do
The Trails End Here and Suicide Sal being testament to that
And so Bonnie and Clyde led the authorities and lawmen on a merry dance
While the ordinary man and woman in the street rooted for them and hoped they'd make it
Because the powers that be had fed them a pack of lies
And sold them all down the river
And every age needs a hero
So it was two years on the run for our mad lovers
Desperate rebels of the last Great Depression
Doomed to die young

130 rounds fired by Frank Hamer's boy's making sure of that
Bonnie screaming in agony as she went down in a hail of bullets
Clyde with his head blown off
The sub-machine guns going rat-a-tat-tat-tat
And afterwards many lesser people accumulating great riches
In the creation and exploitation of the legend
Of Bonnie and Clyde
But that's hardly the point
For with another Great Depression looming
Who will be our new heroes?

Let the Good Times Roll

When the sun shoots into a clear blue sky
And the people look like candy floss
The shack job doesn't seem so bad
The woman proves bearable
The sex is good
And everything feels right
That's the time to
Crack open the booze, swig the vino, raise high the roof beams
Sing rebel songs into a starry night
Climb a mountain
Walk with a lover along a midnight beach
Or cruise the electric city streets till dawn
Looking for a mystery girl
Or even a kiss
For the night was made for god's mad lovers
And young hearts
And the good times won't last forever
So let em roll
Let em roll!

The Kiss

For the dream is a kiss
goodbye
From a street hooker
on a
ragged city street corner
6AM
on a dead
sunday morning
Feeling immortal
and laughing at the sun.

Just another Day in the Cross

Bibi the Brazilian tranny is standing on the corner of Victoria and William
Asking if anyone wants to see a lady
The radio man plotted at the El Alamein fountain
His battered machine eternally tuned to a golden oldies station
The Root, Toot, and Shoot crew are on the nod outside Macdonald's
Performing delicate balancing acts
Like a deranged band of fucked up gymnasts
The two famous bums are sitting in another open-air living room in Barncleuth Square
Two settees, broken TV, coffee table, hat stand, dirty old mattress
Drinking that good cheap port wine and shouting and growling
And smiling at death
Two strippers in the doorway of Playbirds International
Flashing some skin, thighs, cleavage
Juanita, the beautiful but damned aboriginal junky outside the piccolo bar
Waiting to meet her man
The old Chinese Brass licking another 15c cone
Touting for business outside the closed Bureau De Change
A lone and somewhat dispirited spruiker paces the entrance to the Pink Pussy Cat
Smoking a cigarette and scowling a deadbeat scowl
Its forty degrees in the shade
And down at Bondi backpackers are lined up like seals on the beach
And sunny blonde surfer boys and girls are catching blue Pacific Ocean waves
But the Cross is where all the action is
I'm sitting on a bench outside Rite Way
Sucking on an ice-cold longneck of Toohey's Red from a brown paper bag
And taking in the Darlinghurst Scenes
Scribbling notes about everything in an old crumpled notepad

Dreaming of becoming a writer or a poet or something
On the Main Drag
In the last moments of the twentieth century.

To the Girl on the Train

Commuting home on London Underground
Rush hours in the great metropolis
No room to move, no air to breathe
No space to think
City life hell
And then
The vision
Looking straight at me
And I at her
As we hold the gaze
A frozen moment in time
Between two strangers
On a train
She was dressed like someone from the 1930's
Red cheeks and blue eyes
A brunette
And as the carriage rattled
Through those subterranean tunnels
I wondered if I could speak to her
But the idea was impossible
The distance between us
Wider than any ocean.

Great Day

It was the tail end of a four-day bender
On the settee Ronnie asleep for over four hours
Surfer boy standing at the curtains
Muttering something about Old Bill
And imaginary footsteps
Eyes Down in the bedroom
Shagging his fourth brass of the long weekend
In the living room a green television screen
Only one bar working on an electric fire
A coffee table littered with drugs paraphernalia
Cocaine, roaches, speed, pills, beer cans
Even an empty bottle of Drambuie
In the hallway the puppy had pissed and shit everywhere
And devoured my new leather shoes
And a trail of condoms led to the toilet
Which was blocked
And in the kitchen
Water came straight out of a copper pipe
I was lying on the living room floor surrounded
By four kilos of super skunk
A pile of pornographic magazines
And wondering if I could take anymore
When Ronnie suddenly awoke, squinted his eyes, and said
'Great day.'

Australia

In all my time down under
Five years, give and take
I never wrote a single word
Nothing, not even a lousy pome or two
I may have written the odd sporadic letter
Airmail
But that was about the sum of my literary output
I can't even say I was unhappy or frustrated
I was still young
The bars were open 24hrs
And my apartment was surrounding by seven brothels
But somehow, it felt like a time of waiting
Waiting for something happen
I wasn't sure what
But it felt like if I waited long enough
Something eventually would
Happen
So, often I would crack open another bottle of beer
Sit by the window of my apartment
Gaze out on the streets below
And wait, wait, wait.

Zippolite (Beach Poem 17#)

I remember the shattered stars
High above the beach of the dead
The ocean's roar
The gritty sand
The smiling moon
Even the swaying of distant palms
And the girl
Beneath me
And thinking
I will never be this young again

When I Saw Her

It was like an epiphany, an illumination
But instinctively I knew
That she was the one
If there is such a thing as the one
Her pale blue eyes revealed a million sad songs
And to think after all those years
All those lands
All those dreams
There she was standing before me
Making stilted small talk
Nervous and fiercely independent
Yet unafraid to offer me her love.

30

Where did my youth go?
I ask the moon
Whilst atop a WWII pillbox
Drinking beer
On the east coast of England
A waxing moon slung low in the pale evening
Like a discarded smile
And even thou past eleven
A loving hint of daylight remains
Shards of purple across the sky
The tide is out
And a cool breeze blows
One red light sparkling on the horizon
A lone fishing boat
Where did all the years go?
Gone like friends we've lost along the way
Gone like the bars and clubs
Gone like the band at the end of the pier
Gone like girlfriends I will never kiss again
Gone like the blackbird that nested above the wheel of the caravan
Gone like the caravan and the caravan site
Of which nothing remains except the memory of a child's sigh
Gone like the hunchbacked window cleaner
Who walked the streets of my childhood
Like a holy man.

Moonlight in the Gutter

Sadly, a cheap rented room
And moonlight in the gutter
Are all that's left of beauty
When the clock strikes midnight
And an older version of you
Sits at a table
With nothing left but memories.

Ode to the Air-Guitar Busker of Kings Cross

Characters give a place its flavour
Not business people, councillors, community leaders
Or mayors
One such Kings Cross character
Was the air-guitar busker
A homeless man who carried all his
Worldly possessions
In two red and blue striped laundry bags
But who also played air-guitar
He would produce a piece of wood
Hold the stick like a guitar
And strum away
Sometimes for hours on end
He made no sound
He didn't sing
And if you were foolish enough
To toss him a bone
The coin remained wherever it landed
Untouched by the mute busker
Strumming his ax
Who, when finished, would simply put his stick
Back inside his bags
And walk away.

The Corpse

All they found in the room
Was the decomposed body
And blood stains on the carpet
While outside pigeons fucked
Kids screamed
Lovers fought
Car engines roared
Bank robbers struck
Politicians lied
Armies clashed
All of it
And everything
Oblivious to the obscure
Life and death
Of a young woman
And when they removed the corpse
All that was left was the bloodstains on the carpet
And when they removed the carpet
There wasn't even that.

More Beautiful than the Night

The clouds pass, the stars bloom
Blue moonlight across
A sparsely furnished room
Your eyes flashing the eternal gaze
The graceful movement of slender limbs
Red lips pursed on a glamorous cigarette
An attractive plume of purple smoke
The flutter of mascara
Beer can held languidly
Chet Baker on the stereo
A slim volume of poetry by Omar Khayyam
And you, more beautiful than the night.

After Sunrise

Awoke to the sound of waves
The sound of the ocean
A hypnotic eternal rhythm of life
The heartbeat of the planet
Lying in a puddle of cold seawater
Wet and miserable, but also strangely contented
The sun just beginning to rise, a smudge of pink
on the far horizon
Precluding another hot
Stinking day in paradise
From somewhere
The sound of After Sunrise By Sergio Mendes
Drifted hauntingly across the sand
But the party was over
To my left a half-filled bottle of vodka
I reached out to grab it
But only succeeded in knocking it over
Watching impotently as the alcohol poured away
Forever
Then I propped myself up, shielding my vision
By holding a hand to my forehead
And reflected that some lives
Are born to be wasted
Yes, some live are
Born to be wasted.

The Roaring Twenties

I don't know why, but many times
In my twenties
I was plagued by the blue, blues
A black cloud of depression
That followed me around for years
And as most of my twenties
Were spent in Australia
These thoughts often occurred while I pounded
Those sun-baked Sydney streets
Or along those rat-infested alleys of the Cross
Kings Cross
I lived in a succession of beat apartments
Streets I can still recall
Bayswater, Rosyln, Ward, Macleay, Elizabeth, Darlinghurst,
Kellett, Barncleuth, Orwell, Victoria, William, Hughes, McElhone
Interiors I can still recall
Peeling paint, gloomy kitchenettes, poky rooms and rotting bathrooms
And it was always summer, black summer
Hot, dusty streets, tarmac melting in burning sun,
Heat waves shimmering
I was working and drinking, drinking and working
I never wrote anything
But thought about writing, compiling notes and character sketches
Convinced that one day I'd write novels, poems, and short stories
Hundreds of thousand of words describing those
End of century Kings Cross scenes
It was my roaring twenties, but often I felt dead
Everything oppressed me
Work, women, cheap wine, the day to day living
Everyone trying to outdo the other
Petty one-upmanship's
Grubby aspirations
Flawed ambition
The street bums, hookers, and alkis

Seemed more real, open and honest
The tediousness of successful lives always shocked
The monotony and drabness most were prepared to accept
Just to stay alive
Depressed me
But there were few options
People had been dealt a lame hand
By God, Satan, Jesus, science, flashing unknowns
I'd walk to the botanical gardens
And watch the ducks
The life of the average duck appeared
Preferable to the life of the average human being
Sometimes I'd spot a bug walking along a window ledge
And figured I'd rather be a bug
Then I'd walk to the harbour and peer into the depths
Wondering if it was possible to swim away
Into the nothingness of the void
It was my twenties, my roaring twenties
And the world ran away
And the days ran away
And the moon was false and the sun sick
And all that was left was to teeter
On the cusp of the abyss
And smile.

Photograph © by Amber Ace

About the Author

Joseph Ridgwell was raised in East London and is a cult figure of the literary underground both in the UK and abroad. He has published five collections of poetry, two short story collections, three novellas and one novel.

Ridgwell Stories was nominated for a 2016 Pushcart Prize and long-listed for the 2016 Saboteur awards.

A 6th collection of poetry - *Cosmic Gigantic Flywheel* - is due to be published in 2018 by Lenka Editions in Paris.

A 7th Collection of poetry - *The Beach Poems* - will be published by New York's Bottle of Smoke Press in the summer of 2018.

Ridgwell's work has also appeared in numerous anthologies.

For further details of the authors work and current state of mind go to his website: http://josephridgwelljr.wordpress.com/

COLOPHON

This second edition of *where are the rebels?* was published in May 2018 by Ternary Editions. Designed and typeset by Bill Roberts in North Salem, NY. The text is set in Adobe Caslon Pro.

www.ingramcontent.com/pod-product-compliance
Lightning Source LLC
Chambersburg PA
CBHW061345040426
42444CB00011B/3103